Tasty Kernels: Popcorn Recipes for Endless Family Fun

—

Make Movie Night Exciting with a New Recipe Every Time

By Sue Roscoe

Published by MakeRight Publishing, Inc.

ISBN: 978-1074013462

Dedication

I'd like to thank my mom for sharing her love of popcorn with me. And I'd like to thank my husband, Tom, for all of his support and for letting me eat his share of the popcorn.

Table of Contents

Introduction

Welcome to popcorn perfection!

Popcorn can be popped in any number of oils with varying quantities which affect the outcome greatly. Just ask me, I'm a popcorn perfectionado! I grew up loving the stuff and to this day will gladly skip a meal in lieu of a bowl of perfectly popped popcorn. My mom was a single mom and understandably couldn't wait to get all four of us off to bed and turn on the Late Show while enjoying her bowl of popcorn.

The smell of that popcorn would lure me out of my bed and I'd creep back into the living room and peek around the corner. If I was quiet, I could partake. I was quiet. My love of popcorn has followed me through many phases of life and my recipes have adapted through those phases.

Types of Oil to Pop In

The oil you choose has a huge impact on the taste of the final product. No oils are out of bounds. Plain vegetable or corn oil to sunflower, peanut, or canola oils are all standard and the taste between them are similarly delicious. Coconut oil, olive oil and palm oil are some of the best. These oils have a suitable smoke point.

For a more buttery taste, try combining half butter and half oil. This works well in the Whirley Pop Style Popper because of the spinning wire which helps maintain even oil temps and get all the kernels popped. The stainless steel version is the most durable and loved in my kitchen. For something a little more exotic try using duck fat, or bacon fat.

Oil Quantities

While popcorn can be popped in as little as 1, 2, or 3 tablespoons of oil with a half cup popcorn kernels the more you use the more flavor you are imparting to the popcorn. You can even go a step further and use half cup of oil to a third cup of popcorn! By using more oil than corn you will achieve an extra crunchy kernel and added richness.

Cooking Basics

Add oil and popcorn to the pan. Just cover the bottom of the pan in a single layer of kernels with the oil coating the bottom of the pan. Standard recipe is three tablespoons of oil to a half cup of popcorn. Oil quantities can be varied, as mentioned above. Then, place the pan on medium heat and pop with lid on! No peeking, like my sister did, she ended up with a little grease burn right under her eye.

If using a Whirley Pop style popper, begin to turn the wire with the handle, if using a pan agitate the pan gently on occasion. The popping is complete when popping has discontinued, usually taking 2 to 4 minutes, uncover quickly to allow the steam to escape and wait 2 minutes for the corn to crisp before topping further. After topping, get it in the bowl to enjoy!

You'll find the recipes call for sea salt rather than the traditional Kosher salt. We prefer Baja Gold fine for the taste and increased minerals. Feel at liberty to use liberally as it's beneficial for your health.

Almond Butter Popcorn Balls

When you live in the apricot capital of the world you find a lot of uses for dried apricots. Eating a plant-based diet draws your attention to a lot of protein balls and other healthy ingredients. Soon your mixing them together like a mad scientist and rolling them into a ball, coming up with extraordinary combinations and flavors.

INGREDIENTS:

½ cup popcorn kernels
⅓ cup popping oil

1 cup dried apricots
½ cup almond butter
¼ cup almond milk
¼ cup maple syrup
2 tablespoons coconut oil
2 tablespoons flax meal
2 tablespoons ChiliSmith's Lupin Bean Flour or any protein powder
2 teaspoon vanilla extract
Pinch of sea salt

DIRECTIONS:

Pop the popcorn, carefully remove any unpopped kernels and set aside.

In a food processor, process the dried apricots until they are finely chopped. Add the almond butter, coconut oil, almond milk, maple syrup, salt and vanilla extract. Pulse until a liquefied paste forms. Add the Lupin Bean Flour or protein powder, flax seed meal and 4 cups of popped popcorn. Pulse for 5 seconds until the popcorn just breaks down a bit.

Transfer the mixture to a large mixing bowl and with a spatula to incorporate all the ingredients.

With your hands, break the remaining 2 cups of popcorn into finer pieces for about 10 seconds. Form balls (about golf ball size) with the popcorn mixture and dip into the broken popcorn pieces. Form all the mixture into balls. May be stored in fridge for 2 to 3 days or in the freezer for up to a month. Makes one dozen.

Aunt Rosemary and Cousin Garlic Popcorn

These two relatives will *always* be welcome at your family gatherings!

INGREDIENTS:

⅓ cup popcorn kernels
¼ cup olive oil

¼ cup olive oil
3 sprigs rosemary
3 cloves garlic
½ cup parmesan cheese
Sea salt

DIRECTIONS:

Remove rosemary from the stems and finely chop. Press or finely chop the garlic. In a small saucepan warm the first quarter cup olive oil and add your garlic, let it simmer on low for two minutes until you see your garlic browning very lightly then quickly add your rosemary for an additional minute. Remove from heat and set aside.

Pop the corn in the second quarter cup of oil and place in your bowl. Pour your garlic, rosemary oil over the popcorn and toss to coat, add the cheese and any desired salt and toss again. Serve immediately.

Buffalo Wing Popcorn

Hello! I'm Buffalo Wing Popcorn and I need no introduction. To round out your snack buffet serve me with celery stalks and blue cheese. That will mostly be for looks as I'll be the star of the show here, make no mistake about it.

INGREDIENTS:

½ cup popcorn kernels (You'll need 8 popped cups)
⅓ cup popping oil

Nonstick vegetable oil spray
¾ cup sugar
¼ cup Frank's Red Hot Original Sauce
3 tablespoons unsalted butter, cut into pieces
1 teaspoon salt
½ teaspoon baking soda
¼ teaspoon cayenne pepper

DIRECTIONS:

Pop your popcorn and pour out onto the baking sheet to carefully remove unpopped kernels.

Preheat oven to 300°. Spray a baking sheet and a large bowl with nonstick cooking spray. Add popcorn to bowl. Set aside the baking sheet.

Bring sugar and a quarter cup water to a boil in a medium saucepan over medium-high heat, stirring continually. Boil, moving caramel back and forth occasionally, until caramel has darkened, 10 to 12 minutes.

Remove from heat; stir in hot sauce and butter (get ready to see lots of bubbles). Return to a boil and cook another three minutes. Remove from heat; stir in salt, baking soda, and cayenne. Quickly pour your caramel over your popcorn. Caution caramel is hot.

Spread out popcorn on prepared baking sheet and bake, tossing once, until dry, from 15 to 20 minutes. Let cool.

The Classic Caramel Corn

If you'd like to make a new best friend, make up a batch of this and take it to them. That'll do the trick. Makes a lovely Christmas gift in a decorative tin.

INGREDIENTS:

½ cup popcorn kernels (you'll need 8 cups popped)*
⅓ cup popping oil

¾ cup packed brown sugar
6 tablespoons butter
3 tablespoons light corn syrup
¼ teaspoon baking soda
¼ teaspoon vanilla
¼ teaspoon salt
1 cup roasted salted peanuts**

*For best results use a mushroom style popcorn kernel. If unavailable all styles will work.
**Optional: if using just add to popcorn before adding the caramel.

DIRECTIONS:

Carefully remove all unpopped kernels from popped corn. Put popcorn into a 17 x 12 x 2 inch baking pan (or larger). In a 1-½ quart saucepan combine sugar, butter, corn syrup, and ½ teaspoon salt. Cook and stir over medium heat until butter melts and mixture comes to boiling. Cook, without stirring, for five minutes more.

Remove from heat. Stir in baking soda and vanilla. Pour over popcorn; gently stir to coat popcorn. Bake in a 300° oven for 15 minutes, stir. Bake 5 to 10 minutes more. Remove corn to a large bowl or wax paper, lay out on the counter to cool.

Makes 8 cups.

Cheese Please Popcorn

This is hardly a recipe. Actually, it's more of an idea than a recipe but I think it's a good idea and it's one of my personal favorite ways to eat popcorn.

INGREDIENTS:

⅓ cup oil of your choice
½ cup popcorn kernels

3 thick slices of sharp cheddar
3 tablespoons butter melted
Sea salt

DIRECTIONS:

First – and this is very important – get out the cheese and slice it. Next cube it up. You're going to want it to start coming to room temperature, so it softens just a little when it hits the hot popcorn.

Okay, now you're ready. Pop the corn. Place it in the bowl, top it with melted butter, salt it. Now quickly throw the cheese in. Give the bowl a shake to toss the cheese through the top layer just a bit.

It's ready!

Are *you* ready?

Cheesecake Popcorn Cups

Cheesecake, the dream food of royalty!

INGREDIENTS:

⅓ cup popcorn kernels
2 tablespoons popping oil

⅔ cup sugar
2 tablespoons butter
½ cup milk
¾ cup cream cheese
Sea salt
½ teaspoon vanilla
Dash of cinnamon

DIRECTIONS:

Pop the popcorn and set it aside.

Place your butter, sugar and milk in a pan on medium high and bring to boil. Boil for 3 minutes stirring constantly. Remove from heat.

Beat in the cream cheese, vanilla, cinnamon and a pinch of sea salt. Blend until smooth. Pour over prepared popcorn and mix well to coat.

Divide the popcorn between 8 serving dishes and place in the fridge to cool and set completely for 1 to 2 hours. Enjoy within 24 hours.

Chefy Cardamom & Honey Popcorn

Cardamom, with its high end reputation has a slightly exotic flavor profile but really is available to all. It's warm and aromatic flavor adds interest to this slightly sweet popcorn.

INGREDIENTS:

½ cup popcorn kernels (you'll need 8 cups popped)
Oil for popping

5 cardamom seeds - lightly crushed.
3 tablespoons butter
4 tablespoons honey (if it's solid you'll need to warm it up to soften and make it liquid)
Sea salt

DIRECTIONS:

Pop your popcorn and set aside in a large bowl. Melt the butter and add the honey, cardamom seeds and salt. Drizzle over popcorn. Feel a little fancy and enjoy.

Chopstick Cracker Jack

Adding the puffed rice is a really nice change of pace here with this recipe. The five spice is not strong but leaves a wonderful tantalizing taste on your tongue.

You may want to make a double batch as this will be gobbled up in no time. Also makes a great gift and could be packaged and/or served in cute Chinese take-out boxes for an Asian Theme.

INGREDIENTS:

½ cup popcorn
½ cup popping oil

2 cups plain puffed rice
2 cups roasted, salted peanuts
¼ cup black sesame seeds
1 teaspoon five-spice powder
1 cup brown sugar
⅓ cup sorghum
½ teaspoon vanilla extract
½ teaspoon sea salt
¼ teaspoon baking soda
1 stick butter

DIRECTIONS:

First, pop your popcorn.

Preheat the oven to 225 degrees. Line a baking sheet with

parchment paper. Spread the popped popcorn, rice and peanuts evenly on the sheet pan and set aside. In a small bowl, combine the sesame seeds, five-spice powder and baking soda and set aside.

Next, in a heavy-bottomed saucepan, melt the butter over medium heat. Add the brown sugar, sorghum and salt and stir to dissolve. Bring the mixture to a boil and continue to cook until the syrup reaches 250 degrees on a candy thermometer, about 5 minutes. Immediately remove from the heat and add the vanilla extract and sesame seed baking soda mixture. Stir quickly with a wooden spoon to combine.

Finally, pour the hot syrup evenly over the popcorn and nuts. Bake for an hour, stirring every 15 minutes to coat evenly. Remove from the oven and let cool to room temperature. Enjoy.

Churro Popcorn – Yes, I Said Churro Popcorn

If you are having friends over and want to make it easy on yourself, pick up tacos at the local taco truck. Then turn on a movie and wow them with this Churro Popcorn. It comes together in minutes and your hostess skills will get mad props.

INGREDIENTS:

½ cup popcorn kernels (you need about 10 cups)
⅓ cup popping oil

½ cup butter
⅔ cup sugar
3 tablespoons ground cinnamon
2 tablespoons light corn syrup
¼ teaspoon vanilla extract
½ cup powdered sugar
¼ cup sugar
1-½ teaspoon ground cinnamon

DIRECTIONS:

Pop the popcorn, removing all unpopped kernels.

In a small bowl mix together all the ingredients for the churro sugar coating: powdered sugar, granulated sugar and cinnamon.

In a medium saucepan melt butter over medium heat. Add granulated sugar, cinnamon, light corn syrup and vanilla. Allow ingredients to simmer, whisking constantly, until mixture is smooth and no longer grainy, about 2 to 4 minutes.

Pour cinnamon coating over the popped popcorn gently, tossing to coat all. Sprinkle the top of the popcorn with the churro sugar coating. Serve immediately.

Curry Popcorn

This popcorn reminds me of the curry dip my dad first introduced me to as a child. Goes to show you kids can enjoy complex flavors.

This one is a winner in my book.

INGREDIENTS:

¼ cup vegetable oil
½ cup popcorn

½ teaspoon red pepper flakes
½ teaspoon turmeric
1 teaspoon cumin
3 tablespoons butter
Sea salt

DIRECTIONS:

Place your oil and popcorn in your pan. After the first kernel has popped lift the lid, tilting it to protect yourself, quickly add the spices and finish popping. Add melted butter and salt to taste.

Dill and Parm Lived Happily Ever After Popcorn

This recipe brings couples together.

INGREDIENTS:

½ cup popcorn
⅓ cup popping oil

¼ cup grated parmesan cheese
1 teaspoon dried dill
½ teaspoon granulated garlic
3 tablespoons butter
Sea salt

DIRECTIONS:

Mix the dill, parmesan, and garlic together in a small bowl. Pop the popcorn on the stove top in the oil. Remove from pan to a large bowl and salt as desired.

Melt your butter while popping the corn. Distribute melted butter evenly over the popcorn then sprinkle your seasoning over the popcorn.

Everything But the Bagel Popcorn

Add a bunch of seeds and delicious seasonings to your favorite snack to make it an even greater favorite.

INGREDIENTS:

Everything but the Bagel Seasoning (found at Trader Joes) *or* make your own:

1-½ teaspoons poppy seeds
2 teaspoon sesame seeds

½ teaspoon minced dried garlic
1-½ teaspoon minced dried onion
½ teaspoon sea salt
½ cup popcorn kernels
⅓ cup popping oil of your choice
1 garlic clove
4 tablespoons butter

DIRECTIONS:

Mix your Bagel Seasoning together if making your own. Start your butter melting in a small saucepan on low. Mince the garlic and add to the butter.

Pop your corn and remove to a bowl. When your butter is completely melted pour over your popcorn. Then, top with seasoning and add salt as needed.

Genius Apple and Honey Popcorn

The tart apple powder and dash of sweet honey really bring the flavors.

INGREDIENTS:

½ cup popcorn kernels
⅓ cup popping oil

½ ounce freeze dried apples (this is about 2 single serving packs)
⅜ cup coconut oil
½ cup brown sugar
3 tablespoons honey
½ teaspoon baking soda
Pinch of sea salt

DIRECTIONS:

Pop the popcorn and set it aside.

Preheat oven to 350°. Spray two baking sheets with non-stick cooking spray or line with parchment paper.

In a food processor, pulverize the apple crisps until turned into powder. Pour the powder over the popcorn.

Combine the coconut oil, brown sugar and honey in a heavy-bottom saucepan and place on medium high heat. Cook, stirring, until mixture comes to boil. Reduce the heat to a simmer and cook for 3 to 4 minutes, stirring occasionally.

Remove from the heat and stir in the baking soda. The caramel will bubble up and form a smooth, thick foam. Pour this over the popcorn and mix everything together using a large spoon until thoroughly coated.

Caution: The caramel is extremely hot.

Pour onto a baking sheet and bake for 15 minutes or until slightly brown. Cool before breaking into pieces. Store in airtight container.

German Chocolate Popcorn

How could anything with both chocolate *and* coconut *and* popcorn be anything but a taste sensation?

INGREDIENTS:

½ cup popcorn kernels
⅓ cup coconut oil

½ cup sugar
½ cup light corn syrup
½ stick butter
4 tablespoons cocoa powder
1 teaspoon vanilla
Sea salt
3 cups mini marshmallows
½ cup roughly chopped pecans
½ cup toasted sweetened coconut

DIRECTIONS:

Pop the corn and place in large bowl. Remove all unpopped kernels.

In a large pot, bring your cocoa powder, sugar, corn syrup, butter and vanilla to a boil. Add marshmallows, pecans and coconut to the popcorn. Now, stir the melted chocolate mixture and spread out on a parchment lined baking sheet to cool.

Allow to cool and then break into pieces.

Ginger Snap Popcorn

You won't believe how good the traditional ginger snap flavor is on popcorn until you try this.

INGREDIENTS:

½ cup popcorn kernels (12 cups popped corn)
Oil for popping

1 cup toasted sliced almonds
1 teaspoon baking soda
1 teaspoon cinnamon
1 teaspoon ginger
½ teaspoon nutmeg
¼ teaspoon cloves
8 tablespoons unsalted butter
1 cup light brown sugar, lightly packed
2 tablespoons molasses
1 tablespoon water
¼ teaspoon salt
1 teaspoon pure vanilla extract

DIRECTIONS:

Pop the popcorn and carefully remove all unpopped kernels. Toss together the popcorn and almonds in a large bowl; set aside. Spray two large baking sheets with non-stick cooking spray and set aside. Stir together the baking soda, cinnamon, ginger, nutmeg, and cloves in a small bowl; set aside.

Cook the butter, sugar, molasses, water, and salt in a medium-sized, thick-bottomed saucepan over medium heat until the temperature reaches 305°, (hard crack stage), stirring occasionally. Carefully stir in the vanilla and baking soda/spice mix.

Pour caramel over the popcorn stirring to coat popcorn evenly. Spread the popcorn out onto the prepared baking sheets. Let cool before breaking apart.

Green Onion Popcorn

I think Green Onion Seasoning is underused. I prefer it over Ranch. And think this makes a heck of a good bowl of popcorn.

INGREDIENTS:

Green onion seasoning mix packet
Fresh chives

½ cup popcorn kernels
⅓ cup popping oil
3 tablespoons butter

DIRECTIONS:

Pop the corn.

Pour the popped corn into a bowl. Melt the butter. Chop the chives very finely while melting butter. Pour melted butter over popcorn. Top your popcorn with seasoning over popcorn and toss the popcorn in the bowl to evenly distribute. Finish with freshly minced chives. Salt if needed.

Greg's Glazed Donut Popcorn

Greg loves this recipe; as a matter of fact, he loves donuts. Before he travels to a new town he first looks to see if there is a Krispy Kreme Doughnut shop in town. If so, he maps out the route from his hotel to the donut shop.

After he goes to the donut shop he brings his piping hot glazed donuts home and makes this popcorn to munch on all day while he's writing his wonderful books.

It should be obvious: Greg is obsessed with donuts.

INGREDIENTS:

½ cup popcorn kernels
⅓ cup popping oil

4 tablespoons milk
1-½ cups powdered sugar
2 teaspoons vanilla
Pinch of sea salt
7 donut holes or 3 whole glazed donuts
Sprinkles

DIRECTIONS:

First things first, pop the popcorn. Turn the corn out onto a lined baking sheet removing all unpopped kernels. Chop your donuts into bite sized pieces. Warm the milk and vanilla gently on low in a small saucepan and whisk the powdered sugar and salt for the glaze ingredients together until very smooth. Pour over the popcorn. Add your chopped donuts and sprinkles and let cool.

Note: Greg's Glazed Donut Popcorn is best enjoyed the same day but you can store any leftover in an airtight container and eaten the following day.

Halloween Popcorn Brain

Here's a fun and easy popcorn recipe to form into a brain shape, that's super easy to put together and a great way to have some fun with the kids on Halloween.

INGREDIENTS:

½ cup popcorn kernels - 12 cups popped corn
⅓ cup popping oil

Non-stick cooking spray
5 drops green food coloring
3 drops yellow food coloring
4-½ cups marshmallows
½ cup butter
Red twists candy

DIRECTIONS:

Spray large bowl, rubber spatula and piece of waxed paper with cooking spray; set aside. Place 12 cups of popped corn in large bowl, with all unpopped kernels carefully removed.

Microwave the marshmallows and butter in large microwave-safe bowl on *High* for 1 minute and 30 seconds or until the marshmallows melt and mixture blends when stirred. Add food coloring and then stir to combine.

Pour the marshmallow mixture over popped corn. Toss with rubber spatula to coat. Cool five minutes or until mixture is easy to handle. Divide mixture and shape into two "brain lobes."

Place on waxed paper and press lobes together. Cool until set. Transfer to serving platter; decorate with candy, if desired.

Herb Garden Popcorn

We have herbs growing year round in our 700 square foot vegetable garden. The sage, thyme, rosemary and oregano last all year. Running out to the yard and gathering a little handful is such a simple pleasure in life. The freshness brings any dish to life and I secretly feel healthier when I see flecks of green in my food.

This recipe calls for oregano, thyme and rosemary. You could mix it up but I'd add herbs like basil after popping; if wanting to try that. If you don't have outdoor space growing herbs indoors is also easy to do, with kits like Burpee's Indoor Herb Kit and shears bundle, found on Amazon.

INGREDIENTS:

¼ cup olive oil
½ cup popcorn kernels

2 sprigs thyme, rosemary and oregano chopped fine
Sea salt
¼ cup cutter for finishing (optional)

DIRECTIONS:

Chop your herbs finely.

Warm your oil in your saucepan or Whirley Pop to cook your popcorn. Add the herbs and popcorn to the oil and pop as usual.

Top with butter and salt to taste and enjoy.

Honey Mustard Popcorn

Not going to lie, best served with beer. Have some friends over for the game and put this out. They will all be happy!

INGREDIENTS:

½ cup popcorn kernels
¼ cup popping oil

1 stick of butter
1/4 cup honey
1-1/2 tablespoon Dijon mustard
1 tablespoon dried minced onion
1 teaspoon dried mustard
Sea salt
Garlic powder

DIRECTIONS:

Cook popcorn and set aside in large bowl. Preheat oven to 250°. Over medium heat, melt butter and honey. Add the Dijon mustard, bring to simmer. Remove from heat and slowly pour over popcorn. Add onion, dried mustard, salt and garlic powder, stir. Line a baking sheet with parchment and spread out popcorn; bake for 20 minutes stirring occasionally.

Wait for it to cool and enjoy!

Hot Mama Caramel Popcorn

This little spicy number is a great caramel corn with a kick. The thing I like about this recipe is, it does not use corn syrup. You can use it without the cayenne for a regular caramel corn as well. No oven needed.

INGREDIENTS:

½ cup popcorn kernels
Oil for popping

1-½ teaspoons baking soda
¾ teaspoon cayenne pepper
3 cups sugar
½ cup water
3 tablespoons butter
1-½ tablespoons salt

DIRECTIONS:

Pop the corn, removing all unpopped kernels and place in a large mixing bowl or alternatively use a large roasting pan. Spray two spatulas and a large mixing bowl or roasting pan with non-stick cooking spray. Whisk together in a small bowl the cayenne and the baking soda. Get two baking sheets out and have at the ready.

In a medium saucepan, combine the sugar, butter, salt and ½ cup of water. Cook over high heat, without stirring, until the mixture becomes a light golden caramel, 10 to 14 minutes. Remove from the heat and carefully whisk in the baking-soda mixture. The mixture will bubble up.

Pour the caramel mixture over the popcorn in your bowl or roasting pan. I like the roasting pan for this because there is more of a flat surface. Quickly, use the prepared spatulas to toss the caramel and popcorn together, until well coated. Careful, the caramel will be very hot.

Spread the popcorn onto the baking sheets and quickly separate them into small pieces while still warm. Cool to room temperature, about 15 minutes. Once cool, enjoy or store in an airtight container for up to two weeks.

Hurricane Popcorn

This Hawaiian Asian Fusion snack is loved by locals of the Island and eaten often. Once you get your first taste you'll likely find it addictive as well. If you go to a movie theater in Hawaii you may see this offered along with the usual hot buttered popcorn. That's because this snack started from a push cart in Kaneohe.

Now sold prepackaged, we can duplicate it easily with a simple seasoning known as Furikaka, (pronounced *foo-ree-cah-kay*). Nori Furikaka used here has sesame seeds, roasted seaweed, salt and sugar. You can purchase this on Amazon or at a local Asian store near you. Swirl it like a hurricane to mix in the seasoning.

Aloha!

INGREDIENTS:

½ cup unpopped popcorn
⅓ cup popping oil

½ cup of butter
1 tsp. soy sauce
¼ to ½ cup Furikaka (depending on your taste preference)
Rice crackers (optional)

DIRECTIONS:

Cook your popcorn on the stovetop and set aside in a very large bowl.

Melt the butter and add the soy sauce.

Drizzle butter mixture over popcorn and then quickly add your Furikake seasoning and rice crackers if using. Swirl it like a hurricane and enjoy, feeling that laid back island vibe.

Joyful Almond Popcorn

Here's the *best* way we've found to spark joy!

INGREDIENTS:

3 tablespoons coconut oil
½ cup popcorn

1 cup shredded sweetened coconut
¾ cup mini chocolate chips
¾ cup thin sliced almonds
3 tablespoons butter.
Sea salt

DIRECTIONS:

Set your oven to 400°. Toast your coconut on a baking sheet, stirring every minute until brown. On another baking sheet, toast your almond slices in the oven for a minute or two until they show a small amount of color. (Be careful, they cook fast.) Set each aside to cool.

Pop your corn and pour into a large bowl or individual serving bowls. Melt the butter and pour over the popcorn. While the popcorn is warm and buttered, top with your coconut and chocolate chips. The melted butter is optional, but your popcorn will become more cohesive (and flavorful) when you use it.

Loser Cruiser Popcorn Bars

In the days of driving my 15-passenger van, lovingly dubbed as "Loser Cruiser," loaded with my five kids and their friends, I liked to have snacks on hand. These tasty bars with a few healthy ingredients were portable, eased my conscience a little, and worked for us.

INGREDIENTS:

½ cup popcorn kernels - 8 cups popped popcorn
Oil for popping

½ cup sliced almonds
½ cup shredded coconut
½ cup dried apricots
½ cup sweetened dried cranberries
3 tablespoons roasted salted sunflower seeds
⅔ cup butter
¼ cup honey
¼ cup brown sugar
½ teaspoon vanilla
½ teaspoon salt

DIRECTIONS:

Preheat oven to 300°. Spray a 13 x 9 baking pan with non-stick cooking spray and set aside.

Pop your popcorn and remove kernels very carefully. Place popcorn, almonds, coconut, apricots, cranberries and sunflower seeds in a large bowl; set aside.

In a small saucepan, heat the butter, honey, brown sugar, vanilla and salt over medium heat. Stir to blend all ingredients and pour onto baking pan.

With damp hands, press mixture lightly and evenly into pan. Bake 30 minutes until lightly browned. Cool in pan three hours before cutting. You can individually wrap any remainder in plastic wrap and store for two weeks.

Marshmallow Popcorn Treat Bars

This is an improvement on the Cereal Bars we've all come to know and love. For the popcorn lover, there is no need to ask how it's an improvement. If you're like me, you won't be waiting for this to cool down before you're getting your first taste.

INGREDIENTS

½ Cup Popcorn
⅓ Cup Popping Oil

10 oz Mini Marshmallows (Or more if you like them extra gooey as I do)
3 Tablespoons Butter

First pop your popcorn and *remove* the unpopped kernels.

Butter the sides and bottom of 13" x 9" baking dish and set aside. In large pot, melt your marshmallows and butter on medium heat, stirring constantly until completely smooth, about 5 to 7 minutes.

Pour the popcorn into the pan of melted marshmallow mixture. Butter your hands lightly and press coated popcorn into your butter baking dish.

Let cool for a few minutes before cutting and serving the treat bars.

Mexican Hot Chocolate Popcorn

Like spicy? Here's your popcorn!

INGREDIENTS:

3 tablespoons coconut oil (any oil may be substituted)
½ cup popcorn kernels
3 tablespoons butter
½ teaspoon mild chili powder *or* ¼ teaspoon cayenne
3 tablespoons chopped dark chocolate
Sea salt

DIRECTIONS:

Pop the corn in a pan. Melt the butter while the corn pops. Pour popcorn into your bowl. Top with melted butter, salt, chopped chocolate and chili. Toss to coat.

The melted butter is what allows the dry spice to adhere to the popcorn. You'll want the chocolate chopped fairly fine to allow it to soften and meld with the warm popcorn.

Mexican Street (Pop)Corn

I like the savory popcorns. And most everyone likes a little heat. This is so nostalgic of that big piece of corn on the cob with that face licking seasoning all over it! You've just gotta make it.

This one is perfect for the guys and comes together quickly for game day. You won't need much more besides a cold one.

INGREDIENTS:

½ Cup Popcorn (8 cups popped popcorn)
Oil for popping

2 tablespoon butter, melted
2 tablespoon mayonnaise
1 teaspoon lime juice
1 teaspoon salt
1-½ teaspoon paprika
1-¼ teaspoon granulated sugar
⅛ teaspoon ground cayenne pepper

DIRECTIONS:

Pop your popcorn on the stove with plenty of oil so seasoning will stick properly. Set aside in large bowl.

Mix the salt, paprika, sugar and cayenne pepper in a small bowl and have on the ready. Melt the butter and while it is still warm, whisk your mayonnaise and lime juice together.

Pour the butter over your popcorn and quickly add in the seasoning. Toss gently until evenly coated.

Muddy Buddy Popcorn

Great to take to a party and likely to be a repeater.

INGREDIENTS:

⅓ cup popcorn
2 tablespoons oil for popping

1-½ cup powdered sugar
⅓ cup creamy peanut butter
½ cup chocolate chips - semi-sweet or milk chocolate
1 teaspoon vanilla
1 gallon size resealable bag

DIRECTIONS:

Pop your popcorn. Carefully remove all unpopped kernels. This is easier to do this if you pour out the popcorn on a baking sheet. Then pour the popcorn into a large mixing bowl.

Place the powdered sugar in the resealable bag.

In a medium-sized microwaveable bowl, melt the chocolate chips and peanut butter in the microwave, cooking for 30 second intervals and stirring after each interval until the chocolate and peanut butter combination is completely smooth; approximately 90 seconds total. Stir in the vanilla extract.

Pour the melted chocolate over the popcorn and mix with a large rubber spatula until it completely coats each piece of popcorn. Now put that popcorn into the bag of powdered sugar, zip it closed and shake it up. It's ready to serve, store leftovers in an airtight container for up to two days.

Nooch Popcorn

You know, my daughter and I had a bet on how this was pronounced. I'm the kind of girl that does more reading than talking to people and was saying it wrong all the time. The word starts off like new but the ending is "chh" like the ending of pooch. Nooch rhymes with Pooch. Yeah, she won.

If this is all new to you don't be scared. It became my obsession when I was on a vegan phase for about 3 years of my life. I'm no longer in that phase, but this is still my obsession. Nutritional yeast has a unique flavor. Some say it reminds them of parmesan cheese with its nuttiness. I don't make that comparison but just love the stuff.

Oh, and it's full of B Vitamins, protein and fiber. Just give it a try.

INGREDIENTS:

Popcorn
Olive oil

Nutritional yeast
3 tablespoons butter
Sea salt*

*I prefer Baja Gold Fine for its wonderful flavor and texture. Of course the nutritional benefits of the superior quantity of minerals found in this salt over other sea salts.

DIRECTIONS:

Just pop your corn and pour into your bowl. While it's popping, go ahead and melt the butter if your using it. Then dump over the popcorn. While popcorn is still hot, grab a handful of the nutritional yeast and sprinkle over all the popcorn until evenly coated, sprinkle with salt and enjoy this awesome deliciousness.

Nostalgic Pink Popcorn Balls

Did you ever have a Wright's Pink Popcorn when you were little, at such places as the San Francisco Zoo or an amusement park? That's what I would choose when we went to the snack bar. Loved those bricks of popcorn. Just can't explain why.

This recipe takes me right back to those times.

INGREDIENTS:

⅔ cup popcorn kernels
⅓ cup popping oil

1 cup sugar
½ cup light corn syrup
¼ cup butter
1 teaspoon sea salt
½ teaspoon baking soda
1 teaspoon vanilla
1 drop of pink or red food coloring

DIRECTIONS:

Spray a large mixing bowl with non-stick cooking spray. Pop your popcorn and pour it into the bowl you just sprayed. Carefully remove all unpopped kernels.

Combine sugar, corn syrup, butter, and salt in a small, heavy saucepan. Stirring constantly, bring mixture to a boil over medium heat. Continue stirring and boil for two minutes. Remove the sugar mixture from heat and add baking soda, vanilla, and food coloring, stirring until the desired color is reached.

Pour the hot syrup over the reserved popcorn; stir together with a wooden spoon until all the kernels have been well coated. Butter your hands. Working quickly, use your hands to form a 3-inch-diameter ball. Transfer the ball to parchment paper, and let cool completely. Repeat with remaining the popcorn mixture. Wrap individually in plastic wrap or store in an airtight container up to two days.

Introduce these to someone you love and share your memories with them.

Oink Oink Popcorn - Yes! It's Bacon!

It wouldn't be a proper cookbook without bacon.

INGREDIENTS:

½ pound applewood smoked bacon
½ cup popcorn kernels

Oil for popping
3 jalapenos
¼ cup fresh grated parmesan
Sea salt

DIRECTIONS:

Cut your bacon up, about ½ inch pieces will work. Slice your jalapenos thinly into rounds. Cook your bacon in a heavy skillet until crisp. In the last two minute of cooking, add your jalapenos to the pan and cook until you have a little color on them. Remove bacon and jalapenos to a plate lined with paper towels to drain. And get busy on the popcorn.

Cook your popcorn in the oil and pour it into your bowl. While it is still hot, top it with the cheese, jalapenos and bacon. Toss to mix through and salt to taste.

Parmesan Truffle Popcorn

What could be better than a cheesy, truffly flavor?

INGREDIENTS:

½ cup popcorn
⅓ cup popping oil of your choice

2 tablespoons truffle oil
¼ cup butter, melted
1 cup freshly grated parmesan
2 teaspoon finely minced fresh parsley

DIRECTIONS:

Pop the popcorn and pour it out on a baking sheet. Melt the butter and distribute the butter and truffle oil evenly over the popcorn. Sprinkle with parmesan and fresh minced parsley.

Enjoy!

Peanut Butter Marshmallow Popcorn Drool Bars

The actual peanut butter taste in this recipe is not overly strong. It's more of a toffee flavor and if you like marshmallow treats and popcorn you will love this one.

INGREDIENTS:

½ cup popcorn unpopped
⅓ cup oil for popping

¼ cup salted butter
10 ounce bag mini marshmallows
¾ cup Peter Pan simply ground peanut butter or any smooth peanut butter
½ cup chocolate chips

DIRECTIONS:

Pop your corn and set aside in large bowl. This is the time to salt it if desired. Remove all unpopped kernels carefully. Grease a 13 x 9-inch baking dish.

Melt the butter in a large saucepan over medium-low heat until melted. Add the marshmallows and stir until completely melted. Add the peanut butter and stir until it is melted and thoroughly combine the marshmallow mixture.

Now, add the popcorn and quickly stir to coat all of the popcorn.

Pour the popcorn into your prepared baking dish, sprinkle your chocolate chips on top and press down I like to butter my hands and press down but you can keep clean if you like by using a greased spatula. Let cool one hour before cutting.

Pepper Pepper Popcorn Popcorn

I was quite surprised the first time I attended a movie with my friend Sonya to see her ask for peppers with her popcorn at the theater. But actually, in some parts of the U.S., movie theaters serve pepperoncinis or jalapenos with the popcorn if requested and they are complementary. They are smart people who order those peppers.

Why didn't I think of this?

INGREDIENTS:

⅓ cup olive oil
½ cup popcorn

2 jalapeno peppers
Pickled pepperoncinis
2 to 3 tablespoons butter (to taste)
Baja Gold sea salt or salt of your choice

DIRECTIONS:

Pop the popcorn and remove all unpopped kernels.

Slice your jalapenos in wheels. Place then in your popcorn cooking pan with oil and cook on medium for two to three minutes giving them a stir or two from time to time.

Remove the peppers from the oil. Let the oil cool for two to three minutes then add the popcorn. Pop the corn and place in your large bowl. Melt the butter in small saucepan and top the popcorn with melted butter, salt and the jarred sliced pepperoncinis or pickled jalapenos.

Pizza Popcorn

I may be slightly ashamed to admit that pizza and popcorn are my two favorite foods. I don't normally eat them on the same day or at the same time. But there is a way to do it and it's right here.

INGREDIENTS:

½ cup popcorn kernels
⅓ cup olive oil

4 tablespoons butter
¼ cup sun-dried tomatoes in oil, drained well
1 clove garlic, pressed
3 tablespoons grated parmesan
½ teaspoon dried oregano
½ teaspoon dried basil
¼ teaspoon crushed red pepper flake
Sea salt

DIRECTIONS:

Pop your popcorn in your Whirley Pop or heavy bottomed saucepan. Pour into a large bowl. Place the room temperature butter, sun-dried tomatoes and garlic into a food processor and process until smooth. Warm the butter mixture on low heat in a small saucepan until melted; pour over the top of your popcorn. Sprinkle with oregano, basil and parmesan. Salt to taste and serve.

Popcorn Pretzel Toffee Bars

The pretzel bits bring that classic salty hit to this toffee popcorn.

INGREDIENTS:

¼ cup popcorn kernels
Oil for popping

15 graham crackers
1 cup coarsely chopped salted, roasted peanuts
½ cup puffed rice cereal
½ cup chopped pretzel sticks
1-½ cups (3 sticks) butter
¾ cup sugar
6 ounces or 1 cup chopped semisweet or milk chocolate chips

DIRECTIONS:

Pop the popcorn, remove all unpopped kernels carefully and set aside.

Preheat oven to 350°. Line a large baking sheet with foil and spray with nonstick cooking spray. Cover the baking sheet with the graham crackers, breaking as needed to fit the bottom. Top the crackers with the puffed rice, popcorn, pretzels and peanuts.

In a medium saucepan on medium high bring the butter and sugar to a boil. When it boils, give it a stir and reduce the heat to low to maintain a simmer for 8 - 10 minutes. Give a swirl now and then. You are looking for it to become a nice golden brown, thick and syrupy.

Pour the syrup evenly over the bars and bake 10 - 12 minutes until lightly browned. When you bring it out of the oven, sprinkle the chocolate chips evenly over the entire pan. Let it cool before breaking it up. You can store this goodness for up to three days. (If you can get it to last that long.)

Popcorn Trail Mix

Sneak a few healthy ingredients into the popcorn, it's a great little nibble for the kiddos and adults alike.

INGREDIENTS:

¼ cup popcorn kernels
Oil for popping

¼ cup cashews
¼ cup dried sweetened cranberries
3 tablespoons pumpkin or sunflower seeds
2 tablespoons chocolate chips
3 tablespoons raw oats
3 tablespoons melted coconut oil or butter
2 tablespoons honey
½ teaspoon cinnamon
Pinch of salt

DIRECTIONS:

Pop the popcorn and carefully remove unpopped kernels from popcorn. In a large bowl, combine popcorn, cashews, cranberries, seeds, chocolate chips, oats and pinch of salt.

Pour melted coconut oil or butter on top and toss until well combined.

Drizzle honey on top and mix gently until coated. Season with cinnamon and serve.

Pumpkin Caramel Corn

Pumpkin much?

It's either an enthusiastic yes or a hard pass for most people. Pumpkin is a craze for sure, so why not Pumpkin Caramel Corn? This is a no brainer to serve at Halloween or Thanksgiving, well, okay, *any* fall get together.

It's a good thing is you're not restricted just to fall for making it. No one will tell on you. If you do make it in the fall I sure hope you can find some cute little pumpkin containers to serve it in.

INGREDIENTS:

½ cup popcorn kernels
⅓ cup popping oil

½ teaspoon sea salt
½ cup butter
¼ cup light brown sugar, packed
¼ cup light corn syrup
¼ pumpkin puree
¼ teaspoon cinnamon
¼ teaspoon nutmeg
Pinch allspice
¼ teaspoon ground cloves
½ teaspoon vanilla extract
¼ teaspoon baking soda

DIRECTIONS:

Preheat oven to 250°. Line two baking sheets with parchment paper or a silicone baking mat. Set aside. Pop your popcorn and carefully remove any unpopped kernels. Set aside in large bowl.

In a small saucepan over medium heat, melt butter. Mix in brown sugar, pumpkin, corn syrup and spices. When mixture is fully combined and warm, mix in vanilla and baking soda. Mixture should bubble up. Cook for 1 - 2 more minutes, stirring gently. Pour over popcorn, tossing to coat well. Divide caramel corn between prepared pans, being sure to spread out popcorn.

Bake at 250° for 60 minutes, tossing after the first 30 minutes. Remove from oven and immediately break up any clumps. Cool and enjoy. Store in an airtight container.

Sandwich Cookie Popcorn

A sweet treat for the Oreo Cookie Lover.

INGREDIENTS:

½ cup popcorn
⅓ cup popping oil

2 cups white chocolate chips
20 chocolate cream-filled sandwich cookies

DIRECTIONS:

Pop your popcorn in the oil in a large heavy bottomed saucepan or in your Whirley Pop. Pour out onto a baking sheet. Remove all unpopped kernels.

Crush or break the cookies into pieces. Add the cookie crumbs to the popcorn and toss together. Melt your white chocolate chips in a glass bowl in the microwave in 30-second increments. Check and stir every 30 seconds until fully melted. Drizzle the melted white chocolate over the popcorn cookie mixture.

Wait about 40 minutes for it to set.

Tabasco Popcorn

It seems those who like Tabasco *love* Tobasco!

The same holds true for Tabasco Popcorn.

INGREDIENTS:

⅓ cup popcorn kernels
2 tablespoons popping oil
1 tablespoon Tabasco

2 tablespoons honey
2 tablespoons butter
1-½ teaspoon Tabasco
Sea salt

DIRECTIONS:

In a heavy-bottomed skillet with lid or your Whirley Pop, pop your corn with your oil and one tablespoon Tabasco. Put it in a large bowl and salt to taste. Melt your butter in a small saucepan and add the honey and Tabasco. Pour over popcorn and enjoy.

Tajin Popcorn

If you're from my neck of the woods, this one might be a no-brainer. The kids around here put Tajin on their popcorn, on their fruit and just about everything. It's another simple one, but hopefully it inspires you to try.

INGREDIENTS:

½ cup popcorn kernels
⅓ cup popping Oil

Tajin
Sea salt
3 tablespoons butter

DIRECTIONS:

Pop the popcorn. Melt the Butter. Pour the butter over the popcorn in your large bowl. Sprinkle with Tajin and sea salt to taste. Serve it up.

Togarashi Popcorn

Togarashi seasoning is a Japanese seasoning that can be purchased everywhere. Together with the sesame oil you have an exotic savory taste here.

INGREDIENTS:

¼ cup (½ stick) unsalted butter
1 to 3 garlic cloves, minced (to preference)
⅓ cup popcorn kernels
2 tablespoons vegetable oil
1 teaspoon sesame oil
1 teaspoon shichimi togarashi

DIRECTIONS:

Pop the popcorn in vegetable and sesame oil and set aside in large bowl. Melt your butter, adding your minced garlic. Top your popcorn with melted butter and togarashi.

Unicorn Popcorn

Using white popcorn will have a better look when it is sprayed with the pink food spray. You can purchase the food spray and candy melts on Amazon if not found locally.

INGREDIENTS:

⅓ cup white popcorn kernels
Oil for popping

Pink food spray
½ cup pink candy melts
½ cup blue candy melts
2 teaspoons of coconut oil
Pink and blue sprinkles

DIRECTIONS:

Pop your popcorn in the oil in a heavy bottom saucepan or Whirley Pop Popper. Then transfer to two cookie sheets carefully removing all unpopped kernels. Using your pink food spray, spray the popcorn evenly. Cover the baking sheet with another baking sheet and flip over so you can spray the other side.

Allow the popcorn to dry as you prepare the candy melts.

Place each color of candy melts in a small microwave safe bowl with a half teaspoon of coconut oil. Heat for 25 seconds, stir, and reheat as needed. Add in a half teaspoon or more of coconut oil as needed to make the candy melt more liquidy and easy to drizzle.

Drizzle half over the popcorn, add sprinkles, let dry. Reheat the candy melts and toss the popcorn to coat the other side with the second drizzle. Let dry completely

Yin Yang Popcorn

Bet you never thought of using raisins in your popcorn, did ya? It's the sweet (Yin) component that plays off the Yang of the spices.

INGREDIENTS:

¼ cup popcorn kernels
Popping oil

½ cup pecans
2 tablespoons unsalted butter or virgin coconut oil
1 teaspoon ground cinnamon
1 teaspoon kosher salt
1 teaspoon paprika
1 teaspoon ground turmeric
½ teaspoon cayenne pepper
½ teaspoon ground ginger
½ teaspoon ground nutmeg
2 tablespoons pure maple syrup
1 cup golden raisins

DIRECTIONS:

Pop the corn, remove the unpopped kernels and set aside. Melt the butter in a small saucepan, adding all spices. Let cook for about 30 seconds, then remove from heat and add the maple syrup.

Toss your pecans into your popcorn bowl and then top with butter. Place on two baking sheets that you have prepared with cooking spray. Bake at 300° for 30 minutes, turning twice. You are just looking to dry out the popcorn so the seasoning will stick and toast the pecans. When cool, return to bowl and add the raisins.

Enjoy the balanced flavors.

Made in the USA
Columbia, SC
23 June 2019